THE
pressure cooker
COOKBOOK

DEVELOPED BY

**WILLIAMS
SONOMA**

TEST KITCHEN

Photographs Eva Kolenko

weldon**owen**

Contents

Farro Risotto with Mushrooms,
Thyme & Asiago

Lemon-Vanilla Cheesecake
with Berry Compote

All About Pressure Cooking

Here in the Williams Sonoma Test Kitchen, we use pressure cookers to create nutritious, flavorful meals in a flash; from weeknight suppers to weekend dinner parties, it's one of our handiest devices. These appliances cook food more quickly than conventional methods, shaving off huge amounts of time from typically slow-cooking ingredients like dried beans, whole grains, and tough cuts of meat so that meals get on the table faster.

Whether you have a stovetop or an electric model (page 10), they both function the same way: the tightly sealed pot quickly boils liquid, then traps in the steam and generates pressure, so the temperature rises far beyond the boiling point, with the liquid forced into the ingredients, resulting in faster, more evenly cooked food. The high heat of the pressure cooker increases caramelizing and browning, which means that food emerges more flavorful and tender. Dishes that are often reserved for weekends, when they can slow cook all day, can now be made in no time any day of the week.

Discover the impressive speed and efficiency of the pressure cooker through delicious recipes like Green Chile & Tomatillo Carnitas (page 29), Chicken Pho with Lemongrass & Bok Choy (page 14), and Spaghetti Squash with Chicken Meatballs & Quick Tomato Sauce (page 23). You'll also find everyday staples, such as white rice, quinoa, and polenta, which cook in 20 minutes or less and homemade chicken stock (page 59) in just over an hour. Don't forget to save room for dessert. Quick-cooking treats like Coconut & Cinnamon Rice Pudding (page 49) and Salted Dark Chocolate & Amaretto Pots de Crème (page 51) will satisfy any sweet tooth.

Pressure Cooker Features

All of the recipes in this book can be used with either a stovetop or electric pressure cooker. You can read more about the differences between the two models on page 10. Here are just a few of the general features we love about pressure cookers.

Stovetop appliances have easy-to-use pressure valves. You'll know when all the steam has been released because you can actually see and hear the steam while it's being released.

Many appliances include multiple settings for a variety of different dishes. Consult the manufacturer's guide to learn how to best implement individual settings.

One of the advantages of
an electric pressure cooker
is a digital screen that displays
cooking settings and a timer.
Some also have an automatic
steam-release function.

Most stovetop models
are fitted with lock-on lids,
ensuring your safety while
cooking. The lid will click
when properly closed, and
the pressure cooking won't
begin until the lid is locked.

Stovetop & Electric Pressure Cookers

There are two models of pressure cookers: stovetop and electric. Both models come in a variety of sizes; we recommend a 6-quart pot, which cooks 4–6 servings of food and will accommodate all of the recipes in this book. When deciding between pressure cookers, there are a few differences to consider.

Stovetop Pressure Cookers: These models are powered by the heat of a stovetop, which means heat levels are controlled manually. The benefit is that you can use heat, as high as your stovetop will go, to create a perfect sear on meat and poultry before cooking the ingredients under pressure. Generally, these models can reach higher levels of pressure than electric models.

Electric Pressure Cookers: Powered by electricity, these models are portable (you can use them anywhere there's an electrical outlet available) and free up the stovetop for other uses. Built-in timers and preset heat levels that maintain the temperature automatically make electric pressure cookers virtually hands-off. Some models feature no- or low-pressure cooking modes, which means they can also be used as slow cookers.

Consult the manufacturer's guide to learn more about using your device.

What can be cooked in a pressure cooker?

- Bone-in or boneless meat & poultry
- Desserts
- Dips
- Dried beans
- Grains
- Potatoes
- Rice & risotto
- Sauces
- Seafood
- Soups
- Stews
- Stocks
- Vegetables

Natural-Release versus Quick-Release In this book, you will find recipes that call for releasing the steam naturally or quick-releasing the steam. A natural-release is just turning off the heat with a locked lid in place and can take several minutes. A quick-release is when you open the steam valve to release all the steam at once. The method of release is determined by whether a recipe benefits from additional residual cooking by steam (natural-release method), such as grains and beans, or if it's a quick-cooking food that benefits from having all the heat removed at once (quick-release method) so that food doesn't overcook. Consult the manufacturer's guide for more information on releasing steam.

Chipotle Honey Short Ribs

Artichokes Stuffed with Garlicky
Bread Crumbs & Pancetta

Tips & Tricks for Using a Pressure Cooker

Cooking in a pressure cooker is easy, but keeping a few tips and tricks in mind ensures the best-quality results, maintains your pot in tip-top shape, and makes for a safe and seamless experience.

ALWAYS USE LIQUID Pressure cookers work by rapidly bringing liquids to a boil, then trapping the steam to quickly cook the pot's contents. In order for the process to work, all pressure cooker recipes must include liquid; too little liquid can result in dry, overcooked food. Consult the manufacturer's guide to learn about minimum and maximum liquid amounts.

CHOP UNIFORMLY Cut ingredients into roughly the same size so that the food cooks evenly. If preparing a dish that uses both fast- and slow-cooking ingredients (such as potatoes and bone-in beef), partially cook the slow-cooking items first before adding the other ingredients to the pot.

DON'T OVERFILL Leave some room in the pressure cooker for steam to collect and cook the food. Never fill the pot more than two-thirds full with food nor more than half full with liquid.

USE HIGH HEAT Always start pressure cooking on high heat so the contents reach a boil as soon as possible, helping the cooking time to get a jump-start.

KEEP IT CLEAN Although many models are dishwasher-safe, we find that it's easier to wash the cooker, including its hard-to-reach nooks and crannies, by hand. Make sure the appliance is completely dry before storing it.

This icon indicates how much time the recipe takes to cook under pressure.

Steam Safety When releasing pressure and removing the lid from a pressure cooker, it's important to be very cautious as steam is hotter than boiling water and can cause severe burns. To keep your hands safe, use a long-handled wooden spoon or tongs to adjust the valve.

When lifting the pressure cooker lid, wait until the indicator shows the pressure has completely dropped. Then, using pot holders or oven mitts, carefully remove the lid, tilting it away from you to allow the steam to escape. You may need to turn on your kitchen ventilation or open a window to prevent the room from getting too steamy.

Accessories A few recipes call for a trivet and a steamer basket. Most pressure cookers come with these accessories. In place of a trivet, you can use a flat food-grade heatproof item, such as a jar lid, cookie cutter, or upside-down bowl. An ordinary metal kitchen steamer basket works.

Chicken Pho with Lemongrass & Bok Choy

You can cook the stock and chicken for this riff on a Vietnamese favorite up to a couple of days in advance and refrigerate them separately. Then, when it's time to eat, ready the garnishes and finish assembling the soup, and you'll be enjoying supper within just minutes.

3 lb skin-on, bone-in whole chicken legs

Kosher salt

1 tablespoon canola oil

2 yellow onions, quartered

3-inch piece fresh ginger, smashed

6 fresh cilantro sprigs

3 green onions, white and pale green parts, cut into 3-inch pieces

3 lemongrass stalks, white part only, cut into ¼-inch rounds

¼ cup Asian fish sauce, plus more as needed

2 tablespoons firmly packed light brown sugar

2 heads baby bok choy, thinly sliced

8 oz dried rice vermicelli

Garnishes: 3 green onions, thinly sliced; 2 cups mung bean sprouts; 1 cup fresh cilantro leaves; 1 cup torn fresh basil leaves; 2 jalapeño chiles, cut into rings; and 2 limes, cut into wedges

Season the chicken generously with salt. In a pressure cooker pot over high heat, warm the oil. Working in batches, add the chicken and cook until browned on both sides, about 3 minutes per side. Transfer to a plate as browned.

Pour off all but 2 tablespoons of the fat from the pot, add the yellow onions and ginger, and cook, stirring occasionally, until well-browned, 3–5 minutes. Return the chicken to the pot. Add the cilantro, green onions, lemongrass, fish sauce, brown sugar, and 8 cups water and stir to combine.

Lock the lid into place and cook on high pressure for 30 minutes. Quick-release the steam. When the pressure valve drops, remove the lid, tilting it away from your face to allow residual steam to escape.

Transfer the chicken to a cutting board. When it's cool enough to handle, remove the meat, discarding the skin and bones, and shred into bite-size pieces. Pour the stock through a fine-mesh sieve into a large bowl. Discard the solids.

Season the stock with fish sauce as desired. Return the stock to the pressure cooker and bring to a boil, uncovered, over high heat. Add the chicken and bok choy and simmer for 2 minutes. Add the rice vermicelli and simmer until tender, about 3 minutes.

Arrange the garnishes on a platter. Ladle the soup into bowls and serve right away with the garnishes alongside.

SERVES 4

Cooking times for
rice noodles vary,
so follow the package
instructions.

Kalua-Style Pork with Cabbage

If desired, cook the pork the day before, reserving the liquid for cooking the cabbage just before serving. Refrigerate separately. Remove the solidified fat from the top of the liquid, then melt the fat in a large sauté pan and warm the shredded pork until the edges are crispy.

Place the bacon slices in a single layer in a pressure cooker pot and cook over medium heat until the fat starts to render, about 3 minutes. Turn off the heat and flip the slices over.

Season the pork generously with salt (about 2 tablespoons per piece of pork). Place the pork on top of the bacon and add 1 cup water.

Lock the lid into place and cook on high pressure for 1 hour. Let the steam release naturally, about 15 minutes. When the pressure valve drops, remove the lid, tilting it away from your face to allow residual steam to escape.

Transfer the pork and bacon to a large bowl and shred with 2 forks. Cover with aluminum foil to keep warm. Adjust the seasoning with salt. Add the cabbage wedges to the liquid in the pot. Lock the lid into place and cook on high pressure for 4 minutes. Quick-release the steam. Using tongs, transfer the cabbage to a bowl. Serve the pork over the cabbage and garnish with green onions.

SERVES 6–8

¼ lb sliced bacon

4 lb boneless pork shoulder, trimmed and cut into 3-inch pieces

Kosher salt

1 head red cabbage, cut into 8 wedges

Thinly sliced green onions, green parts only, for garnish

Brisket Sandwiches with Horseradish Crème Fraîche

Brisket is sold in two cuts—flat cut and point cut. Select the flat cut, which is easier to slice once cooked, and look for brisket with deep, rich color and generous, even white marbling, qualities that ensure a moist, succulent finish.

1 beef brisket (about 2½ lb)

Kosher salt and freshly ground pepper

3 cloves garlic, grated

1 tablespoon Worcestershire sauce

1 tablespoon vegetable oil

½ cup red wine

1 yellow onion, thinly sliced

2 cups Chicken Stock (page 59) or beef stock

½ cup barbecue sauce

1 tablespoon firmly packed light brown sugar

1 tablespoon Dijon mustard

2 fresh thyme sprigs

2 tablespoons all-purpose flour

½ cup crème fraîche

2 teaspoons prepared horseradish

8 thick slices brioche or 4 brioche buns, toasted

Coleslaw and pickles, for serving (optional)

Let the brisket stand at room temperature for 30 minutes. Pat dry and season generously with salt and pepper. In a small bowl, whisk together the garlic and Worcestershire sauce. Brush the fat side of the brisket with the mixture.

In a pressure cooker pot over medium-high heat, warm the oil. Add the brisket, fat side up, and cook until browned, about 3 minutes. Transfer to a plate.

Reduce the heat to medium, add the wine to the pot, and cook, stirring to scrape up the browned bits. Add the onion, stock, barbecue sauce, brown sugar, mustard, and thyme and stir to combine. Return the brisket to the pot, fat side up.

Lock the lid into place and cook on high pressure for 1 hour. Let the steam release naturally, about 15 minutes. When the pressure valve drops, remove the lid, tilting it away from your face to allow residual steam to escape.

Transfer the brisket to a cutting board, tent with aluminum foil, and let rest for 5 minutes before thinly slicing against the grain. Continue to cook the liquid uncovered over medium-high heat until it begins to simmer. Whisk in the flour and simmer until the gravy has thickened, about 10 minutes. Remove and discard the thyme sprigs.

Meanwhile, in a small bowl, whisk together the crème fraîche and horseradish and season with salt and pepper. To assemble each sandwich, spread the horseradish crème fraîche on a slice of brioche. Add a few slices of brisket and spoon some gravy over the meat. Top with coleslaw and pickles, if using. Cover with another brioche slice and serve.

SERVES 4

Try using fresh horseradish: peel the skin, then use a microplane to grate. Stir 2 teaspoons into the crème fraîche.

Jambalaya with Andouille Sausage

This staple of the Louisiana Creole table is loaded with vegetables, protein, and rice, making it an ideal one-pot meal. Offer chopped fresh cilantro for garnish and serve with a green salad and a white Sancerre or Sauvignon Blanc.

1 lb skinless, boneless chicken thighs, cut into 1-inch pieces

Kosher salt and freshly ground pepper

6 tablespoons vegetable oil

¾ lb smoked andouille sausage, cut diagonally into ¼-inch slices

1 large yellow onion, coarsely chopped

3 cloves garlic, minced

1 *each* large red and green bell pepper, seeded and coarsely chopped

2 ribs celery, cut diagonally into ½-inch slices

2½ teaspoons Old Bay seasoning

1 teaspoon garlic powder

½ teaspoon *each* dried thyme and smoked paprika

1½ cups long-grain white rice

2 tablespoons tomato paste

1 can (28 oz) crushed tomatoes

1½ cups Chicken Stock (page 59)

Season the chicken with salt and pepper. In a pressure cooker pot over medium-high heat, warm 3 tablespoons of the oil. Working in batches, add the chicken and cook until browned on both sides, about 1 minute per side. Transfer to a plate as browned.

Add the sausage to the pot and cook, stirring frequently, for 1 minute. Add the onion, garlic, bell peppers, and celery and drizzle with the remaining 3 tablespoons oil. Add the Old Bay seasoning, garlic powder, thyme, and paprika and stir to combine. Cook, stirring occasionally, until the vegetables soften slightly, about 3 minutes. Add the rice, tomato paste, tomatoes, stock, and reserved chicken and bring to a boil.

Lock the lid into place and cook on high pressure for 8 minutes. Let the steam release naturally, about 5 minutes. When the pressure valve drops, remove the lid, tilting it away from your face to allow residual steam to escape.

Continue to cook, uncovered, over medium heat, stirring frequently, until slightly thickened, about 5 minutes. Ladle the jambalaya into bowls and serve.

SERVES 4–6

Clam Chowder with Potatoes, Leeks & Bacon

Elevate this dish by using 1½ lb fresh clams. To prepare, steam the clams in a single layer in a pan with ½ cup each white wine and water over medium-low heat until they open, 5–10 minutes. Shell and use only the open clams.

In a pressure cooker pot over medium heat, cook the bacon, stirring occasionally, until crispy and the fat is rendered, about 5 minutes. Stir in the leeks and a pinch each of salt and pepper. Add the wine and cook, stirring to scrape up the browned bits. Add the potatoes, bay leaf, thyme, and 2½ cups water.

Lock the lid into place and cook on high pressure for 5 minutes. Let the steam release naturally, about 5 minutes. When the pressure valve drops, remove the lid, tilting it away from your face to allow residual steam to escape.

Remove and discard the bay leaf and thyme sprigs. In a small saucepan over medium heat, whisk together the butter and flour, stirring constantly, and cook until the roux is lightly toasted, about 2 minutes. Stir the roux, milk, and cream into the pressure cooker pot. Continue to cook, uncovered, over medium heat until thickened, about 5 minutes. Stir in the clams and cook until warmed through.

Ladle the chowder into bowls and top with a grinding of pepper and the parsley. Serve right away.

SERVES 4

½ lb bacon, diced

3 leeks, white and pale green parts, thinly sliced

Kosher salt and freshly ground pepper

½ cup white wine

3 Yukon gold potatoes, peeled and cut into ½-inch pieces

1 bay leaf

2 fresh thyme sprigs

1 tablespoon unsalted butter

1 tablespoon all-purpose flour

1 cup whole milk

1 cup heavy cream

2 cans (6½ oz each) clams, drained

2 tablespoons chopped fresh flat-leaf parsley

When spaghetti squash is out of season, use zucchini instead and cut it with a spiral vegetable slicer or julienne peeler and cook in salted water.

Spaghetti Squash with Chicken Meatballs & Quick Tomato Sauce

To form equal-size and perfectly round meatballs, use an ice-cream scoop and then gently roll the mixture between your palms. You can replace the ground chicken with ground turkey or pork; use darker cuts of meat for optimal flavor.

Make the tomato sauce and spaghetti squash.

In a large frying pan over medium-high heat, warm 2 tablespoons of the oil. Add the onion and cook, stirring occasionally, until softened, about 3 minutes. Add the garlic and cook, stirring occasionally, until fragrant, about 1 minute. Transfer to a small bowl and let cool. Wipe out the pan.

Line a baking sheet with parchment paper. In a large bowl, combine the egg, bread crumbs, cheese, basil, red pepper flakes, salt, black pepper, chicken, and onion mixture. Mix gently with your hands until the ingredients are incorporated. Form the mixture into twelve 2-inch balls and place on the prepared baking sheet.

Warm the remaining 3 tablespoons oil in the frying pan over medium heat. Working in batches, add the meatballs and cook until browned on all sides, about 1 minute per side.

Pour the tomato sauce into the pressure cooker pot. Add the meatballs and coat in the sauce. Lock the lid into place and cook on high pressure for 5 minutes. Quick-release the steam. When the pressure valve drops, remove the lid, tilting it away from your face to allow residual steam to escape.

Meanwhile, microwave the spaghetti squash until warmed through, 3–5 minutes. Serve the meatballs and sauce over the spaghetti squash. Garnish with cheese, basil, and red pepper flakes.

SERVES 4–6

1 recipe Quick Tomato Sauce (page 61)

1 recipe Spaghetti Squash (page 61)

5 tablespoons olive oil

1 small yellow onion, chopped

3 cloves garlic, minced

1 large egg, lightly beaten

½ cup dried bread crumbs

½ cup grated Parmesan cheese, plus more for garnish

3 teaspoons chopped fresh basil, plus leaves for garnish

2 teaspoons red pepper flakes, plus more for garnish

3 teaspoons kosher salt

2 teaspoons freshly ground black pepper

1 lb ground dark-meat chicken

Shrimp Risotto with Lemon & Basil

If you like risotto but don't like to stand and stir for a half hour, this recipe is for you. Once the stock goes into the pot, the pressure cooker does all of the work, leaving you only to stir in the butter and cheese just before serving.

4 tablespoons olive oil

1 yellow onion, diced

2 cups Arborio rice

¼ cup white wine

4 cups vegetable stock
or Chicken Stock (page 59)

1 lb medium shrimp,
peeled and deveined

Kosher salt and freshly
ground pepper

3 cloves garlic, minced

1 tablespoon unsalted butter

½ cup grated
Parmesan cheese

2 teaspoons grated
lemon zest

¼ cup slivered fresh basil

In a pressure cooker pot over medium heat, warm 2 tablespoons of the oil. Add the onion and cook, stirring occasionally, until softened, about 3 minutes. Add the rice and cook, stirring occasionally, until toasted, about 3 minutes. Add the wine and cook, stirring to scrape up the browned bits, then stir in the stock.

Lock the lid into place and cook on high pressure for 7 minutes. Let the steam release naturally, about 5 minutes. When the pressure valve drops, remove the lid, tilting it away from your face to allow residual steam to escape.

Meanwhile, pat the shrimp dry and season generously with salt and pepper. In a large sauté pan over high heat, warm the remaining 2 tablespoons oil. Add the garlic and shrimp and cook, turning once, until golden brown and opaque, about 2 minutes per side. Set aside.

Stir the butter and cheese into the risotto and season with salt and pepper. Transfer to a serving platter or divide among 4 bowls. Top with the shrimp, lemon zest, and basil and serve right away.

SERVES 4

For a one-pot dish, don't sear the shrimp; instead, stir them into the cooked risotto and cook, uncovered, until pink and opaque.

30 minutes

Ginger Pork Stew with Potatoes

Take the time to brown the pork before adding the other ingredients. The caramelization that results from this step deepens the flavor and enriches the stew's color. Pass slices of country bread for sopping up the delicious sauce.

3 lb boneless pork shoulder, trimmed and cut into 1½- to 2-inch pieces

Kosher salt and freshly ground pepper

6 tablespoons vegetable oil, plus more as needed

1 yellow onion, chopped

3 cloves garlic, minced

2 tablespoons peeled and minced fresh ginger

2 tablespoons minced lemongrass, white part only

1 serrano chile, seeded and finely chopped

1½ teaspoons ground coriander

1½ teaspoons dry mustard

1 cup Chicken Stock (page 59)

1 can (13.5 fl oz) coconut milk

1 Asian eggplant, cut into 2-inch pieces

1½ lb Yukon gold potatoes, cut into 2-inch pieces

2 red bell peppers, seeded and cut into 2-inch pieces

¼ cup chopped fresh cilantro

Fresh lime juice, for garnish

Season the pork generously with salt and pepper. In a pressure cooker pot over medium-high heat, warm 3 tablespoons of the oil. Working in batches, add the pork and cook until browned on all sides, about 1 minute per side. Transfer to a plate as browned.

Return the pork to the pot and add the remaining 3 tablespoons oil. Add the onion, garlic, ginger, lemongrass, and serrano and cook, stirring occasionally, until slightly softened, 3–5 minutes. Add the coriander, mustard, 3 teaspoons salt, and 1 teaspoon pepper and stir to combine.

In a medium bowl, whisk together the stock and coconut milk and pour into the pot. Add the eggplant, potatoes, and bell peppers and stir to combine.

Lock the lid into place and cook on high pressure for 15 minutes. Quick-release the steam. When the pressure valve drops, remove the lid, tilting it away from your face to allow residual steam to escape.

Ladle the stew into bowls, garnish with the cilantro and lime juice, and serve.

SERVES 4

Spicy Chickpeas with Radish-Cilantro Yogurt

To release the full flavor of mustard seeds, fry them in hot oil, covered, until they pop. When the popping subsides, quickly uncover and add the other ingredients as directed to prevent the seeds from burning.

In a pressure cooker pot over medium-high heat, warm the oil until shimmering. Add the mustard seeds and cumin seeds, cover, and fry until the mustard seeds begin to pop, about 30 seconds.

When the popping subsides, quickly remove the lid, reduce the heat to medium, and add the onion. Cook, uncovered, stirring occasionally, until softened, about 5 minutes. Add the garlic, ginger, jalapeño, coriander, garam masala, turmeric, paprika, and 1 teaspoon salt and cook, stirring frequently, until fragrant, about 2 minutes. Add the chickpeas, tomatoes with their juices, and ½ cup water and stir to combine.

Lock the lid into place and cook on high pressure for 8 minutes. Quick-release the steam. When the pressure valve drops, remove the lid, tilting it away from your face to allow residual steam to escape.

Meanwhile, in a medium bowl, stir together the yogurt, radishes, cilantro, and lime juice. Season with salt and pepper.

Adjust the seasoning of the chickpeas with salt and serve over white rice. Top with a dollop of the radish-cilantro yogurt and garnish with cilantro leaves.

SERVES 4

2 tablespoons canola oil

1 teaspoon black mustard seeds

1 teaspoon cumin seeds

½ yellow onion, diced

2 cloves garlic, minced

1 tablespoon peeled and finely grated fresh ginger

1 jalapeño chile, seeded and finely diced

2 teaspoons ground coriander

1 teaspoon garam masala

1 teaspoon ground turmeric

½ teaspoon smoked paprika

Kosher salt and freshly ground pepper

1 recipe Chickpeas (page 58) or 2 cans (15½ oz *each*) chickpeas, drained and rinsed

1 can (15 oz) diced tomatoes with juices

¾ cup plain Greek yogurt

4 radishes, coarsely grated

¼ cup chopped fresh cilantro, plus whole leaves for garnish

1 teaspoon fresh lime juice

1 recipe White Rice (page 55), for serving

Before cutting into tomatillos, be sure to remove and discard the rough husks.

Green Chile & Tomatillo Carnitas

Whip up a batch of your favorite guacamole to serve with this flavorful, meltingly tender pork. If you like your food spicy, leave some or all of the seeds in the chiles. At the table, offer guests cold beer or a seasonal agua fresca.

In a large bowl, combine the pork, 3 teaspoons salt, 3 teaspoons pepper, the coriander, cumin, paprika, and garlic powder. Using your hands, coat the pork evenly with the spices.

In a pressure cooker pot over medium-high heat, warm 3 tablespoons of the oil. Working in batches, add the pork and cook until browned on all sides, about 1 minute per side. Transfer to a plate as browned.

Warm the remaining 3 tablespoons oil in the pot over medium-high heat. Add the serranos, jalapeño, tomatillos, onion, and garlic and cook, stirring occasionally, until softened, about 3 minutes. Add 2 teaspoons salt and the stock and bring to a boil. Return the pork to the pot and stir to coat.

Lock the lid into place and cook on high pressure for 1 hour. Quick-release the steam. When the pressure valve drops, remove the lid, tilting it away from your face to allow residual steam to escape.

Transfer the pork to a large bowl, and using 2 forks, shred the pork. Add the sauce to the pork and stir to incorporate. Serve in tortillas or over rice with serranos, crème fraîche, cilantro, and lime wedges alongside.

SERVES 4–6

---

3 lb boneless pork shoulder, trimmed and cut into 3-inch pieces

Kosher salt and freshly ground pepper

2 teaspoons ground coriander

2 teaspoons ground cumin

1 teaspoon smoked paprika

½ teaspoon garlic powder

6 tablespoons vegetable oil

2 serrano chiles, seeded and chopped, plus more for serving

1 jalapeño chile, seeded and chopped

5 tomatillos, husked, cored, and diced

1 yellow onion, diced

4 cloves garlic, minced

1 cup beef stock

Warmed corn tortillas or cooked rice, for serving

Crème fraîche, for serving

Fresh cilantro leaves, for serving

Lime wedges, for serving

Chipotle Honey Short Ribs

These hot-sweet ribs are especially satisfying on chilly evenings. Make sure to buy ribs with a thick layer of meat, passing up ribs cut from the flank end, which are typically more lean.

1 chopped chipotle chile in adobo sauce, plus 3 tablespoons adobo sauce

1 cup honey

Juice of 1 lime

2 tablespoons Dijon mustard

1½ teaspoons garlic powder

¼ cup tomato paste

¼ cup Chicken Stock (page 59)

Kosher salt and freshly ground pepper

5 lbs bone-in beef short ribs

¼ cup vegetable oil, plus more as needed

1 recipe Polenta (page 57), for serving

Chopped fresh flat-leaf parsley, for serving

In a bowl, whisk together the chipotle chile and adobo sauce, honey, lime juice, mustard, garlic powder, tomato paste, and stock. Season with salt and pepper. Set the sauce aside.

Pat the short ribs dry and season generously with salt and pepper. In a pressure cooker pot over medium-high heat, warm the oil. Working in batches, add the short ribs and cook until browned on both sides, 1–2 minutes per side. Transfer to a plate as browned. If the meat begins to stick, add up to 3 tablespoons more oil. Return the short ribs, meat side down, to the pot. Pour the sauce over the ribs, using tongs to stir and coat each rib.

Lock the lid into place and cook on high pressure for 45 minutes. Quick-release the steam. When the pressure valve drops, remove the lid, tilting it away from your face to allow residual steam to escape.

Transfer the short ribs to a platter. Continue to cook the sauce uncovered over medium-high heat until it begins to boil. Reduce the heat to medium-low and simmer until the sauce has thickened slightly and darkened in color, about 5 minutes. Serve the short ribs over polenta, spoon the sauce on top, and garnish with parsley.

SERVES 4–6

To boost the heat,
finely chop 1 or 2
more chipotle chiles
in adobo and add
to the sauce.

To prevent trimmed artichokes from turning brown, submerge them in a bowl of lemon water or rub the trimmed parts with a lemon half.

Artichokes Stuffed with Garlicky Bread Crumbs & Pancetta

Preparing this Southern Italian classic in a pressure cooker ensures the artichokes are cooked to a uniformly tender finish. Serve them as a first course, followed by a simple roasted meat, or as a light main, accompanied with olive oil–dressed roasted peppers.

In a food processor, process the bread until fine crumbs form. Transfer to a large frying pan and add the oil. Place over medium heat and cook, stirring occasionally, until golden brown, about 6 minutes. Remove from the heat and stir in the garlic and lemon zest. Season with salt and pepper. Transfer the crumbs to a bowl and wipe out the pan.

In the same frying pan over medium heat, cook the pancetta, stirring occasionally, until crispy, about 6 minutes. Add to the bread crumb mixture and stir to combine. Set aside.

Working with 1 artichoke at a time, cut off the stem flush with the bottom and discard, then cut 1 inch off the top. Using scissors, trim the leaves so the tips are straight and scoop out the choke from the center. Season the inside of the artichokes with salt and pepper. Divide the bread crumb mixture evenly among the artichokes, packing it firmly into the center where the choke was removed. Sprinkle the cheese on top of the filling, dividing evenly. Place the artichokes, filling side up, in a pressure cooker pot and add the wine and 2½ cups water.

Lock the lid into place and cook on high pressure for 10 minutes. Let the steam release naturally, about 5 minutes. When the pressure valve drops, remove the lid, tilting it away from your face to allow residual steam to escape.

Transfer the artichokes to a serving platter and serve warm.

SERVES 4

2 cups country bread pieces, crusts removed

¾ cup olive oil

3 cloves garlic, minced

2 teaspoons grated lemon zest

Kosher salt and freshly ground pepper

¼ lb pancetta, chopped

4 large artichokes

½ cup grated Parmesan cheese

½ cup white wine

Eggplant Spread with Olives & Fresh Thyme

Caramelizing the eggplant in a little oil develops a smoky flavor, and finishing the cooking on high pressure makes quick work of preparing this Middle East–inspired spread.

---

2 lb eggplant

5 tablespoons olive oil, plus more as needed

Kosher salt and freshly ground pepper

4 cloves garlic, unpeeled

⅓ cup fresh lemon juice

2 tablespoons tahini

½ cup pitted Kalamata olives, chopped, plus more for garnish

1 tablespoon chopped fresh thyme, or 3 tablespoons chopped fresh flat-leaf parsley, plus more for garnish

4–6 pita bread rounds, each cut into 8 wedges

Using a vegetable peeler, peel the eggplant in alternating stripes, with skin and no skin, then cut into large chunks. In a pressure cooker pot over medium heat, warm the oil. Working in batches, add the eggplant and cook, turning the pieces occasionally with tongs, until beginning to smoke slightly and caramelize, about 4 minutes. Transfer to a plate as browned. Add more oil between batches if needed. Return the eggplant to the pot and season generously with salt and pepper. Add the garlic and 1–3 cups water, depending on the size of your cooker. Meanwhile, preheat the oven to 375°F. Line a baking sheet with aluminum foil.

Lock the lid into place and cook on high pressure for 3 minutes. Quick-release the steam. When the pressure valve drops, remove the lid, tilting it away from your face to allow residual steam to escape.

Using a slotted spoon, remove the garlic cloves and squeeze the flesh into a food processor. Using the slotted spoon, transfer the eggplant to the processor. Add the lemon juice, tahini, olives, and thyme and process until smooth, about 2 minutes. Transfer the eggplant spread to a serving bowl and let cool to room temperature.

Place the pita wedges on the prepared baking sheet, drizzle with oil, and season with salt and pepper. Bake until golden brown and crispy on the edges, 8–10 minutes.

When ready to serve, drizzle the eggplant spread with oil and garnish with olives and thyme. Serve the pita toasts alongside.

SERVES 4–6

For a different, chunky texture, skip the food processor and mash the eggplant and garlic mixture with a large whisk or potato masher, then stir in the remaining ingredients.

Smoky Black Bean Soup with Cilantro-Lime Crema

To add meat and more smokiness to this robust vegetarian soup, coarsely dice 1 pound chorizo, kielbasa, or andouille and add with the seasonings. For a soup and sandwich supper, opt for grilled cheese made with pepper Jack.

1 tablespoon canola oil

1 yellow onion, diced

1 red bell pepper, seeded and diced

1 jalapeño chile, seeded and minced

3 cloves garlic, minced

1 tablespoon adobo sauce from canned chipotles

1 tablespoon ground cumin

1½ teaspoons smoked paprika

1 teaspoon dried oregano

Kosher salt and freshly ground pepper

1 lb (about 2½ cups) dried black beans, picked over and rinsed

4 cups vegetable stock

1 cup sour cream

¼ cup chopped fresh cilantro, plus more for garnish (optional)

¼ cup minced red onion

1 teaspoon grated lime zest

2 tablespoons fresh lime juice

In a pressure cooker pot over medium heat, warm the oil. Add the yellow onion and bell pepper and cook, stirring occasionally, until softened, about 5 minutes. Add the jalapeño, garlic, adobo sauce, cumin, paprika, oregano, and 1 teaspoon salt and cook, stirring occasionally, until fragrant, about 2 minutes. Add the beans and stock and stir to combine.

Lock the lid into place and cook on high pressure for 45 minutes. Let the steam release naturally, about 15 minutes. When the pressure valve drops, remove the lid, tilting it away from your face to allow residual steam to escape.

Meanwhile, in a bowl, stir together the sour cream, cilantro, red onion, lime zest, and 1 tablespoon of the lime juice. Season with salt and pepper.

Stir the remaining 1 tablespoon lime juice into the soup and adjust the seasoning with salt and pepper. Ladle the soup into bowls and top each portion with a large spoonful of the cilantro-lime crema. Garnish with more cilantro, if using, and serve right away.

SERVES 6

Duck Legs Braised with Garlic & Rosemary

Instead of cooking duck legs low and slow to tenderize them and infuse them with flavor, use your pressure cooker. To boost the vegetable component, add a couple of handfuls of pearl onions along with the carrots.

Pat the duck legs dry with paper towels and season generously with salt and pepper. In a pressure cooker pot over medium-high heat, warm the oil. Add the duck, skin side down, and cook until golden brown, about 3 minutes. Transfer to a plate.

Pour off all but 1 tablespoon of the fat from the pot. Reduce the heat to medium and add the garlic. Cook, stirring occasionally, until fragrant, about 1 minute. Add the wine and cook, stirring to scrape up the browned bits. Add the stock, carrots, and rosemary sprigs and stir to combine. Return the duck legs, skin side up, to the pot.

Lock the lid into place and cook on high pressure for 20 minutes. Let the steam release naturally, about 10 minutes. When the pressure valve drops, remove the lid, tilting it away from your face to allow residual steam to escape.

Transfer the duck and carrots to a platter and sprinkle the duck with the chopped rosemary. Serve over potatoes.

SERVES 6

2½ lb duck legs

Kosher salt and freshly ground pepper

1 tablespoon olive oil

4 cloves garlic, thinly sliced

½ cup white wine

2½ cups Chicken Stock (page 59)

4 carrots (about 1 lb total weight), peeled and thinly sliced

2 fresh rosemary sprigs, plus 2 teaspoons finely chopped fresh rosemary

Quick-Steamed Potatoes (page 54), for serving

Fingerling Potato Salad with Radishes & Dill

The pressure cooker is a great way to cook hard-boiled eggs. The yolks and whites emerge evenly cooked, and the eggs are much easier to peel than eggs cooked the conventional way. If you cannot find fingerling potatoes, use small white, red, or new potatoes.

In a medium bowl, stir together the onion and 3 tablespoons of the vinegar. Let stand until the onion softens slightly, about 5 minutes. In a small bowl, whisk together the remaining 1 tablespoon vinegar, the oil, and mustard. Stir into the onion mixture and season with salt and pepper. Set aside.

Place a trivet on the bottom of a pressure cooker pot, place a steamer basket on top, and pour in 3 cups water. Arrange the potatoes in a single layer in the basket. Nestle the eggs on top of the potatoes.

Lock the lid into place and cook on high pressure for 8 minutes. Let the steam release naturally, about 5 minutes. When the pressure valve drops, remove the lid, tilting it away from your face to allow residual steam to escape.

Transfer the eggs to a bowl of cold water and let cool to room temperature. Transfer the potatoes to a large bowl. Add the radishes and the vinaigrette and toss to combine. Season with salt and pepper. Peel the eggs and cut into ¼-inch slices. Top the potato salad with the eggs and dill. Serve warm or at room temperature, or refrigerate up to overnight and serve chilled.

SERVES 6

½ red onion, thinly sliced

4 tablespoons red wine vinegar

¼ cup olive oil

2 tablespoons Dijon mustard

Kosher salt and freshly ground pepper

3 lb fingerling potatoes, cut into 2-inch pieces

2 large eggs

6 radishes, thinly sliced

2 tablespoons coarsely chopped fresh dill

Farro Risotto with Mushrooms, Thyme & Asiago

Be sure to purchase semipearled (*semiperlato*) farro rather than whole-grain farro, which requires both soaking and different timing. Serve the risotto alongside grilled lamb rib or loin chops and sautéed greens, and uncork your favorite Cabernet Sauvignon.

---

4 tablespoons olive oil

½ lb wild mushrooms, such as king trumpets or maitakes, brushed clean and thinly sliced

1 yellow onion, diced

1½ cups semipearled farro

½ cup white wine

3 cups vegetable stock or Chicken Stock (page 59), plus more as needed

2 tablespoons finely chopped fresh thyme

1 tablespoon unsalted butter

¼ cup grated Asiago cheese

Kosher salt and freshly ground pepper

In a frying pan over medium-high heat, warm 2 tablespoons of the oil. Add the mushrooms and cook, stirring occasionally, until golden brown and tender, about 4 minutes. Set aside.

In a pressure cooker pot over medium heat, warm the remaining 2 tablespoons oil. Add the onion and cook, stirring occasionally, until softened, about 3 minutes. Add the farro and cook, stirring occasionally, until toasted, about 3 minutes. Add the wine and cook, stirring to scrape up the browned bits, then stir in the stock.

Lock the lid into place and cook on high pressure for 8 minutes. Let the steam release naturally, about 5 minutes. When the pressure valve drops, remove the lid, tilting it away from your face to allow residual steam to escape.

Stir the thyme and mushrooms into the risotto. Continue to cook, uncovered, over medium heat, stirring frequently, until the risotto has thickened, about 3 minutes, adding more stock if the risotto becomes too thick. Stir in the butter and cheese. Season with salt and pepper and serve right away.

SERVES 4

To vary the flavor, try using fresh rosemary or sage in place of the thyme, and pecorino or Gruyere for the Asiago.

For a classic pairing, serve this rich, hearty sauce on wide, flat fresh or dried tagliatelle.

Bolognese with Red Wine & Sage

If desired, garnish the sauce with fried sage leaves: In a small saucepan over medium heat, melt 2 tablespoons butter and cook until it begins to foam, about 1 minute. Add whole fresh sage leaves and fry for 30 seconds per side. Transfer to paper towels to drain and sprinkle with salt right away.

In a pressure cooker pot over medium-high heat, cook the bacon, stirring occasionally, until crispy and the fat is rendered, about 5 minutes. Add the butter, onion, carrot, and celery and cook, stirring occasionally, until softened, about 5 minutes. Add the beef, pork, and sage and cook, breaking up the meat with a wooden spoon, until browned, about 5 minutes. Add the wine and cook, stirring to scrape up the browned bits, for 3 minutes. Add the tomato paste, tomatoes, 3 teaspoons salt, and 3 teaspoons pepper and stir to combine.

Lock the lid into place and cook on high pressure for 8 minutes. Quick-release the steam. When the pressure valve drops, remove the lid, tilting it away from your face to allow residual steam to escape.

Continue to cook, uncovered, over medium heat until the sauce has thickened, about 10 minutes. Stir in the cream and cheese. Serve over pasta and garnish with more cheese.

SERVES 4

---

5 oz bacon slices, diced

3 tablespoons unsalted butter

1 yellow onion, finely chopped

1 carrot, peeled and finely chopped

1 rib celery, finely chopped

1 lb ground beef

1 lb ground pork

1 tablespoon chopped fresh sage

⅓ cup red wine

1 tablespoon tomato paste

1 can (15 oz) crushed tomatoes

Kosher salt and freshly ground pepper

2 tablespoons heavy cream

1 cup grated Parmesan cheese, plus more for garnish

Cooked pasta, for serving

French Onion Soup with Gruyère Crostini

This bistro mainstay traditionally calls for an hour or more of nearly constant stirring on the stovetop before the stock is even added. But this pressure cooker version dramatically reduces both the time and the cook's labor, making it a good choice for a weeknight dinner.

½ cup unsalted butter

3 lb yellow onions, sliced ⅛ inch thick

½ teaspoon baking soda

Kosher salt and freshly ground pepper

½ cup dry sherry, such as amontillado

2 cups Chicken Stock (page 59)

3 fresh thyme sprigs

1 bay leaf

2 teaspoons cider vinegar

Juice of ½ lemon

1 baguette, cut into ½-inch slices

1 clove garlic, halved lengthwise

1 lb Gruyère cheese, grated

Minced fresh chives, for garnish

In a pressure cooker pot over medium heat, melt the butter. Add the onions and baking soda and stir to combine. Season generously with salt and pepper. Cook, stirring occasionally, until the onions soften slightly and start to release their liquid, about 3 minutes.

Lock the lid into place and cook on high pressure for 20 minutes. Let the steam release naturally, about 5 minutes. When the pressure valve drops, remove the lid, tilting it away from your face to allow residual steam to escape.

Continue to cook, uncovered, over medium heat, stirring constantly, until the liquid has reduced slightly and the onions have darkened and caramelized, 5–7 minutes. Add the sherry, bring to a simmer, and cook, stirring gently, until the alcohol has evaporated, about 3 minutes. Add the stock, thyme, bay leaf, vinegar, and lemon juice, reduce the heat to medium-low, and simmer for 10 minutes.

Meanwhile, preheat the oven to 375°F. Line a baking sheet with aluminum foil. Place the baguette slices on the prepared baking sheet. Rub the top of each slice with the cut side of the garlic and bake the crostini for 5 minutes. Sprinkle generously with the cheese. Bake until the cheese is melted and just beginning to brown, about 3 minutes.

Season the soup with salt and pepper. Remove and discard the thyme sprigs and bay leaf. Ladle the soup into bowls, garnish with chives, and serve with the crostini.

SERVES 4–6

Chicken Noodle Soup with Leeks & Parsnips

Chicken thighs have a richer, fuller flavor than chicken breasts, so don't be tempted to use chicken breasts in this classic. Select wide, sturdy egg noodles that will marry well with the hearty vegetables and shredded chicken. If parsnips are unavailable, turnips are a good substitute.

Season the chicken with salt and pepper. In a pressure cooker pot over high heat, warm the oil. Working in batches, add the chicken and cook until browned on both sides, about 3 minutes per side. Transfer to a plate as browned.

Pour off all but 2 tablespoons of the fat from the pot. Reduce the heat to medium and add the parsnips, leeks, celery, and onion. Cook, stirring occasionally, until softened, about 5 minutes. Add the garlic and thyme and cook, stirring occasionally, until fragrant, about 30 seconds. Return the chicken to the pot and add the stock.

Lock the lid into place and cook on high pressure for 20 minutes. Let the steam release naturally, about 15 minutes. When the pressure valve drops, remove the lid, tilting it away from your face to allow residual steam to escape.

Meanwhile, cook the egg noodles according to the package instructions and drain.

Transfer the chicken to a cutting board. When cool enough to handle, remove the meat, discarding the skin and bones, and shred into bite-size pieces. Return the chicken to the pot. Continue to cook, uncovered, over medium-high heat until warmed through. Add the lemon juice and Worcestershire sauce. Adjust the seasoning with salt and pepper.

Divide the egg noodles among individual bowls and ladle the soup on top. Garnish with parsley and serve right away.

SERVES 4–6

---

3 lb skin-on, bone-in chicken thighs

Kosher salt and freshly ground pepper

1 tablespoon olive oil

4 parsnips (about 1 lb total weight), peeled and diced

3 leeks, white and pale green parts, halved lengthwise and thinly sliced

2 ribs celery, sliced

½ yellow onion, diced

2 cloves garlic, minced

1 teaspoon minced fresh thyme

8 cups Chicken Stock (page 59)

½ lb egg noodles

1 tablespoon fresh lemon juice

1 tablespoon Worcestershire sauce

Chopped fresh flat-leaf parsley, for garnish

Turkey Chili with Mushrooms & Zucchini

Chili recipes are easy to customize, including this one. Try trading out the turkey for dark-meat chicken, the shiitakes for cremini mushrooms, and the zucchini for your favorite summer squash. Serve corn bread alongside.

---

6 tablespoons olive oil, plus more as needed

2 lb ground dark-meat turkey

Kosher salt and freshly ground pepper

1 small yellow onion, diced

2 cloves garlic, minced

¾ lb shiitake mushrooms, brushed clean, stemmed, and caps sliced

3 zucchini, halved lengthwise and cut into 1-inch slices

1 can *each* (15 oz) white beans, chickpeas, pinto beans, and corn, drained and rinsed

1 can (28 oz) crushed tomatoes

2 teaspoons *each* ground cinnamon and ground cumin

1½ teaspoons chipotle chile powder

1 teaspoon dry mustard

Shredded Cheddar cheese, for serving

Chopped fresh flat-leaf parsley, for serving

In a pressure cooker pot over medium-high heat, warm 3 tablespoons of the oil. Add the turkey and season with salt and pepper. Cook, breaking up the meat with a wooden spoon, until lightly browned, about 5 minutes. Transfer to a bowl.

Warm the remaining 3 tablespoons oil in the pressure cooker pot over medium-high heat. Add the onion and garlic and cook, stirring occasionally, until softened, about 3 minutes. Add the mushrooms and zucchini and cook, stirring occasionally, for 1 minute. If the vegetables begin to stick to the pot, add up to 2 tablespoons more oil. Reduce the heat to low and add the turkey, the white and pinto beans, chickpeas, corn, tomatoes, cinnamon, cumin, chile powder, mustard, and 3 teaspoons each salt and pepper and stir to combine.

Lock the lid into place and cook on high pressure for 8 minutes. Quick-release the steam. When the pressure valve drops, remove the lid, tilting it away from your face to allow residual steam to escape.

Continue to cook, uncovered, over medium heat, stirring occasionally, until the chili has thickened slightly, 5–8 minutes. Ladle the chili into bowls and garnish with cheese and parsley.

SERVES 6

Swap the Cheddar for
your favorite cheese,
like crumbled feta or
queso fresco.

55 minutes

Tomato-Braised Lamb Shoulder with Mint

Accompany this hearty Mediterranean stew, flavored with mint, oregano, garlic, and lemon, with a spinach salad or vinaigrette-dressed green beans. If you can't find boned lamb shoulder, buy and debone lamb shoulder chops.

---

2 lb boneless lamb shoulder, cut into 2-inch cubes

Kosher salt and freshly ground pepper

1 tablespoon olive oil

1 yellow onion, diced

3 cloves garlic, minced

1 tablespoon dried mint

1 teaspoon dried oregano

1 teaspoon grated lemon zest

½ cup Kalamata olives, pitted and coarsely chopped

1 can (28 oz) diced tomatoes with juices

¼ cup chopped fresh mint, plus torn leaves for garnish

1 recipe Polenta (page 57), for serving

Season the lamb generously with salt and pepper. In a pressure cooker pot over medium-high heat, warm the oil. Working in batches, add the lamb and cook until browned on all sides, about 3 minutes per side. Transfer to a plate as browned.

Add the onion to the pot and cook, stirring occasionally, until softened, about 5 minutes. Add the garlic, dried mint, oregano, and lemon zest and cook, stirring occasionally, until fragrant, about 30 seconds. Return the lamb to the pot and stir in the olives and tomatoes with their juices.

Lock the lid into place and cook on high pressure for 25 minutes. Let the steam release naturally, about 10 minutes. When the pressure valve drops, remove the lid, tilting it away from your face to allow residual steam to escape.

Stir in the chopped fresh mint and adjust the seasoning with salt and pepper. Serve the lamb and sauce over polenta and garnish with torn mint leaves.

SERVES 4

Coconut & Cinnamon Rice Pudding

The addition of the eggs to the cooked rice not only adds extra richness but also gives this pudding a custardy texture and turns it a lovely pale yellow. If serving the dessert chilled, top each portion with a few blueberries.

In a pressure cooker pot over medium-high heat, combine the rice, sugar, cinnamon, 1 teaspoon salt, and the milk and bring to a boil, stirring constantly to dissolve the sugar.

Lock the lid into place and cook on low pressure for 18 minutes. Turn off the heat and wait for 10 minutes, then quick-release the steam. When the pressure valve drops, remove the lid, tilting it away from your face to allow residual steam to escape.

In a bowl, whisk together the eggs, half-and-half, and vanilla and coconut extracts and stir into the rice. Continue to cook, uncovered, over medium heat, stirring occasionally, until the mixture just begins to boil. Turn off the heat and stir in the shredded coconut.

Serve the pudding warm, sprinkled with cinnamon and shredded coconut. Or, divide the pudding among individual bowls and let cool completely, then cover and refrigerate for up to 3 days. Just before serving, sprinkle with cinnamon and shredded coconut.

SERVES 6–8

1½ cups Arborio rice

1 cup sugar

3 teaspoons ground cinnamon, plus more for garnish

Kosher salt

5 cups whole milk

2 large eggs

¾ cup half-and-half

1½ teaspoons pure vanilla extract

2 teaspoons coconut extract

½ cup unsweetened shredded coconut, plus more for garnish

For a silky-smooth texture, strain the mixture through a fine-mesh sieve before pouring into ramekins. Try swapping the amaretto for another liquor, such as bourbon.

Salted Dark Chocolate & Amaretto Pots de Crème

Add the hot cream mixture to the beaten eggs slowly and whisk constantly to ensure no bits of yolk coagulate. When adding the chocolate, continue to whisk steadily but gently, or you will create foam that can result in an uneven surface when the mixture sets.

In a saucepan over low heat, combine the cream and milk and bring to a simmer. Meanwhile, in a large bowl, whisk together the egg yolks, sugar, ½ teaspoon kosher salt, and the amaretto. Whisk the hot cream mixture into the egg yolk mixture until combined. Slowly add the chocolate and whisk until melted and completely smooth. Divide evenly among six 4-oz ramekins.

Place a trivet on the bottom of a pressure cooker pot, place a steamer basket on top, and pour in 2 cups water. Place the ramekins in the steamer basket in a single layer. Cook them in batches, if needed.

Lock the lid into place and cook on high pressure for 6 minutes. Let the steam release naturally, about 5 minutes. When the pressure valve drops, remove the lid, tilting it away from your face to allow residual steam to escape.

Carefully remove the ramekins from the pot. Repeat the process if cooking in batches.

When all are cooked, let cool to room temperature, cover with plastic wrap, and refrigerate until set, at least 2 hours or up to 3 days. Just before serving, sprinkle with sea salt and top with a dollop of whipped cream.

SERVES 6

1 cup heavy cream

1 cup whole milk

5 large egg yolks

⅓ cup sugar

Kosher salt

3 tablespoons amaretto

½ lb semisweet chocolate chips

Sea salt, for garnish

Whipped cream, for serving

Lemon-Vanilla Cheesecake with Berry Compote

To move the cake pan in and out of the pressure cooker, create a foil sling: Fold a long piece of foil in half lengthwise a few times. Center the pan on the sling and use the ends to move it. Keep the sling in place during cooking.

---

1 recipe Berry Compote (page 54)

6 oz graham crackers

4 tablespoons unsalted butter, melted and cooled

1 lb cream cheese, at room temperature

¾ cup sugar

¼ cup sour cream, at room temperature

2 large eggs, at room temperature

1 tablespoon *each* grated lemon zest and juice

1 teaspoon pure vanilla extract

1 vanilla bean, split and seeds scraped, with seeds reserved

Make the berry compote.

Line an 8-inch round cake pan with aluminum foil, extending the lining 2 inches above the sides of the pan. In a food processor, pulse the graham crackers until fine crumbs form. Add the butter and pulse until the mixture comes together. Press the graham cracker mixture into the bottom and about ¼ inch up the sides of the prepared pan. Set aside.

In the bowl of a stand mixer fitted with the paddle attachment, beat together the cream cheese, sugar, and sour cream on medium speed until smooth, about 3 minutes. Stop the mixer and scrape down the sides of the bowl. Add the eggs, lemon zest and juice, vanilla extract, and vanilla bean seeds and beat on medium-high speed until combined, about 1 minute. Pour the filling into the crust. Place a trivet in the pressure cooker, pour 3 cups water into the pot, and place the cake pan on the trivet.

Lock the lid into place and cook on high pressure for 15 minutes. Let the steam release naturally, about 10 minutes. When the pressure valve drops, remove the lid, tilting it away from your face to allow residual steam to escape. Carefully remove the cake pan from the pot and refrigerate in an airtight container until set, at least 2 hours or up to 3 days.

Serve the cheesecake topped with the berry compote.

SERVES 8

Substitute fresh lime juice and zest for the lemon and/or add ½ teaspoon ground ginger to the crust mixture.

Berry Compote

20 minutes

In a pressure cooker pot, combine the strawberries, blackberries, sugar, and lemon juice.

Lock the lid into place and cook on high pressure for 3 minutes. Let the steam release naturally, about 5 minutes. When the pressure valve drops, remove the lid, tilting it away from your face to allow residual steam to escape.

Continue to cook, uncovered, over high heat, stirring occasionally, until the berry mixture begins to boil. Meanwhile, in a small bowl, whisk together the cornstarch and 1 tablespoon water. Reduce the heat to medium and stir in the cornstarch mixture. Cook, stirring frequently, until the compote has thickened, about 5 minutes. Let cool completely before serving or transfer to an airtight container and refrigerate for up to 1 week.

2 cups strawberries, fresh or frozen

1 cup blackberries, fresh or frozen

¾ cup sugar

2 tablespoons fresh lemon juice

1 tablespoon cornstarch

MAKES ABOUT 2 CUPS

Quick-Steamed Potatoes

8 minutes

Place a trivet on the bottom of a pressure cooker pot and pour in 2 cups water. Put the potatoes in a steamer basket and set it on the trivet.

Lock the lid into place and cook on high pressure for 8 minutes. Quick-release the steam. When the pressure valve drops, remove the lid, tilting it away from your face to allow residual steam to escape.

Transfer the potatoes to a serving bowl. Season with salt and pepper and serve or use as desired.

2 lb russet or Yukon gold potatoes, cut into 2-inch cubes

Kosher salt and freshly ground pepper

SERVES 4–6

White Rice

In a pressure cooker pot, combine the rice, 1 teaspoon salt, and 1¼ cups water. Lock the lid into place and cook on high pressure for 3 minutes. Let the steam release naturally, about 10 minutes. When the pressure valve drops, remove the lid, tilting it away from your face to allow residual steam to escape. Fluff the rice with a fork and serve or use as desired.

 13 minutes

1 cup long-grain
white rice, rinsed

Kosher salt

MAKES 2½ CUPS

Brown Rice

In a pressure cooker pot, combine the rice, 1 teaspoon salt, and 1¼ cups water. Lock the lid into place and cook on high pressure for 17 minutes. Quick-release the steam. When the pressure valve drops, remove the lid, tilting it away from your face to allow residual steam to escape. Fluff the rice with a fork and serve or use as desired.

 17 minutes

1 cup brown rice, rinsed

Kosher salt

MAKES 2½ CUPS

Wild Rice

In a pressure cooker pot, combine the rice, 1 teaspoon salt, and 3 cups water. Lock the lid into place and cook on high pressure for 30 minutes. Quick-release the steam. When the pressure valve drops, remove the lid, tilting it away from your face to allow residual steam to escape. Fluff the rice with a fork and serve or use as desired.

 30 minutes

1 cup wild rice, rinsed

Kosher salt

MAKES 2½ CUPS

Polenta

Quinoa

Brown Rice

Lentils

Wild Rice

White Rice

Quinoa

 12 minutes

In a pressure cooker pot, combine the quinoa, 1 teaspoon salt, and 1½ cups water. Lock the lid into place and cook on high pressure for 2 minutes. Let the steam release naturally, about 10 minutes. When the pressure valve drops, remove the lid, tilting it away from your face to allow residual steam to escape. Fluff the quinoa with a fork and serve or use as desired.

1 cup quinoa, rinsed

Kosher salt

MAKES 2½ CUPS

Polenta

 18 minutes

In a pressure cooker pot over high heat, combine the liquid and 2 teaspoons salt and bring to a boil. Slowly stream in the polenta, whisking constantly so it does not clump.

Lock the lid into place and cook on high pressure for 8 minutes. Quick-release the steam. When the pressure valve drops, remove the lid, tilting it away from your face to allow residual steam to escape.

Season the polenta with salt and pepper. Stir in the butter and cheese, if using, and serve.

4 cups liquid (water, whole milk, and/or chicken stock)

Kosher salt and freshly ground pepper

1 cup polenta

2 tablespoons unsalted butter (optional)

½ cup grated Parmesan cheese (optional)

MAKES 2½ CUPS

Cannellini Beans

 40 minutes

In a pressure cooker pot, combine the beans, oil, and 4 cups water. Lock the lid into place and cook on high pressure for 30 minutes. Let the steam release naturally, about 10 minutes. When the pressure valve drops, remove the lid, tilting it away from your face to allow residual steam to escape. If the beans are not yet tender, lock the lid into place and cook on high pressure for 3–5 minutes longer. Season with salt and serve or use as desired.

1 cup dried cannellini beans, sorted and rinsed

1 teaspoon canola oil

Kosher salt

MAKES 2½ CUPS

Black Beans

In a pressure cooker pot, combine the beans, oil, and 4 cups water. Lock the lid into place and cook on high pressure for 28 minutes. Let the steam release naturally, about 10 minutes. When the pressure valve drops, remove the lid, tilting it away from your face to allow residual steam to escape. If the beans are not yet tender, lock the lid into place and cook on high pressure for 3–5 minutes longer. Season with salt and serve or use as desired.

 40 minutes

1 cup dried black beans, sorted and rinsed

1 teaspoon canola oil

Kosher salt

MAKES 2½ CUPS

Chickpeas

In a pressure cooker pot, combine the chickpeas, oil, and 4 cups water. Lock the lid into place and cook on high pressure for 35 minutes. Let the steam release naturally, about 10 minutes. When the pressure valve drops, remove the lid, tilting it away from your face to allow residual steam to escape. If the chickpeas are not yet tender, lock the lid into place and cook on high pressure for 3–5 minutes longer. Season with salt and serve or use as desired.

 45 minutes

1¼ cups dried chickpeas, sorted and rinsed

1 teaspoon canola oil

Kosher salt

MAKES 3½ CUPS

Lentils

In a pressure cooker pot, combine the lentils, oil, and 4 cups water. Lock the lid into place and cook on high pressure for 15 minutes. Let the steam release naturally, about 10 minutes. When the pressure valve drops, remove the lid, tilting it away from your face to allow residual steam to escape. If the lentils are not yet tender, lock the lid into place and cook on high pressure for 3–5 minutes longer. Season with salt and serve or use as desired.

 25 minutes

1 cup green or brown lentils, sorted and rinsed

1 teaspoon canola oil

Kosher salt

MAKES 2½ CUPS

Chicken Stock

 1 hour 20 minutes

Season the chicken with the salt. In a pressure cooker pot over high heat, warm the oil. Working in batches, add the chicken and cook until browned on both sides, about 3 minutes per side. Transfer to a plate as browned.

Add the onion and carrots to the pot and cook, stirring occasionally, until browned, about 2 minutes. Add 1 cup water and cook, stirring to scrape up the browned bits. Return the chicken to the pot and add the parsley, thyme, bay leaves, garlic, peppercorns, and 11 cups water.

Lock the lid into place and cook on high pressure for 45 minutes. Let the steam release naturally, about 15 minutes. When the pressure valve drops, remove the lid, tilting it away from your face to allow residual steam to escape.

Pour the stock through a fine-mesh sieve into a large bowl. Discard the solids. Let the stock cool completely, then ladle into airtight storage containers. Refrigerate for up to 1 week or freeze for up to 3 months.

3 lb chicken parts (drumsticks, backs, necks, and wings)

2 teaspoons kosher salt

1 tablespoon olive oil

1 yellow onion, quartered

2 carrots, cut into 3-inch pieces

3 fresh flat-leaf parsley sprigs

3 fresh thyme sprigs

2 bay leaves

2 cloves garlic, smashed

¼ teaspoon whole black peppercorns

MAKES 3 QUARTS

Spaghetti Squash with Chicken Meatballs
& Quick Tomato Sauce

Spaghetti Squash

 10 minutes

Place a trivet on the bottom of a pressure cooker pot and pour in 3 cups water. Place the squash halves, cut side down, in a steamer basket and set it on the trivet. Lock the lid into place and cook on high pressure for 4–6 minutes (about 2 minutes per lb). Let the steam release naturally for 3 minutes, then quick-release the steam. When the pressure valve drops, remove the lid, tilting it away from your face to allow residual steam to escape.

Transfer the squash to a cutting board. Gently run a fork along the inside of the squash to scrape the flesh free from the skin and transfer the strands to a microwave-safe bowl. Drizzle the squash with oil and season with salt and pepper. Serve warm with your favorite sauce.

1 medium spaghetti squash (2–3 lb), halved widthwise and seeded

Olive oil, for drizzling

Kosher salt and freshly ground black pepper

SERVES 4–6

Quick Tomato Sauce

 10 minutes

In a pressure cooker pot, whisk together the stock, tomatoes, tomato paste, basil, oregano, red pepper flakes, oil, mustard, and ½ teaspoon each salt and black pepper until well combined.

Lock the lid into place and cook on high pressure for 5 minutes. Let the steam release naturally, about 5 minutes. When the pressure valve drops, remove the lid, tilting it away from your face to allow residual steam to escape. Adjust the seasoning with salt and pepper. Serve, or let cool completely and transfer to an airtight container and refrigerate for up to 1 week.

2 cups Chicken Stock (page 59)

1 can (28 oz) crushed tomatoes

½ cup tomato paste

1 tablespoon chopped fresh basil

2 teaspoons dried oregano

3 teaspoons red pepper flakes

¼ cup olive oil

1 tablespoon Dijon mustard

Kosher salt and freshly ground black pepper

MAKES ABOUT 4 CUPS

Index

The Pressure Cooker Cookbook

Conceived and produced by Weldon Owen, Inc.
in collaboration with Williams Sonoma, Inc.
3250 Van Ness Avenue, San Francisco, CA 94109

A WELDON OWEN PRODUCTION
1045 Sansome Street, Suite 100
San Francisco, CA 94111
www.weldonowen.com

WELDON OWEN, INC.
President & Publisher Roger Shaw
SVP, Sales & Marketing Amy Kaneko
Finance & Operations Director Philip Paulick

Associate Publisher Amy Marr
Associate Editor Emma Rudolph

Creative Director Kelly Booth
Art Director Marisa Kwek

Printed in China
First printed in 2016
10 9 8 7 6 5

Production Director Chris Hemesath
Associate Production Director Michelle Duggan
Imaging Manager Don Hill

Library of Congress Cataloging-in-Publication
data is available.

ISBN: 978-1-68188-217-8

Photographer Eva Kolenko
Food Stylist Lillian Kang
Prop Stylist Alessandra Mortola

Weldon Owen is a division of Bonnier Publishing USA

ACKNOWLEDGMENTS

Weldon Owen wishes to thank the following people for their generous support
in producing this book: Kris Balloun, Lesley Bruynesteyn, Gloria Geller,
Veronica Laramie, Elizabeth Parson, Nik Sharma, Sharon Silva, and Xi Zhu